PLAY BY PLAY

FIELD EVENTS

DISCARD

Thanks to Richfield coaches Pat Burns
and Kyle Infozato and the following
athletes who were photographed for
this book:
Pat Akappate
Megan Bielefeld
Pat Doty
Jeff Dowell
Nate Fias
Rachel Gieseke
Nikki Jensen
Ben Johnson
Mike Johnson
Ona Johnson
Robin Lass
Erin Petrik
Megan Petrik
Svetlana Sinykin
Brie Waltman

LERNER
SPORTS
AN IMPRINT OF LERNER PUBLISHING GROUP
www.lernerbooks.com

PLAY BY PLAY

FIELD EVENTS

Kristin Wolden Nitz

Photographs by Andy King

L

LernerSports • Minneapolis

For Mom and Dad

This book is available in two editions:
Library binding by LernerSports
Soft cover by LernerSports • FAE
Imprints of Lerner Publishing Group
241 First Avenue North
Minneapolis, MN 55401 U.S.A.

Website address: www.lernerbooks.com

Library of Congress Cataloging-in-Publication Data

Nitz, Kristin Wolden.
  Play-by-play field events / by Kristin Wolden Nitz;
photographs by Andy King.
    p.   cm. — (Play-by-play)
  Includes index.
  Contents: How this sport got started—Getting started—The long jump—The triple jump—The high jump—The pole vault—The shot put—The discus—The meet.
  ISBN: 0–8225–3933–0 (lib. bdg. : alk. paper)
  ISBN: 0–8225–9874–4 (pbk. : alk. paper)
  1. Track and field—Juvenile literature. [1. Track and field.] I. King, Andy, ill. II. Title. III. Series.
GV1060.55 .N58 2004
796.42—dc21   2002152925

Manufactured in the United States of America
1 2 3 4 5 6 – JR – 09 08 07 06 05 04

Photo Acknowledgments
Additional photographs are reproduced with the permission of: © Hulton|Archive by Getty Images, p. 6; © Bettmann/CORBIS, pp. 7, 10, 39 (top and middle), 67; © Philip Gould/CORBIS, p. 8; © Gianni Dagli Orti/CORBIS, p. 9; © SportsChrome East/West, Louis A. Raynor, p. 11; © Wally McNamee/CORBIS, p. 22; © Library of Congress, p. 25; © Hulton-Deutsch Collection /CORBIS, p. 39 (bottom); © S. Carmona/CORBIS, p. 43; © AFP/CORBIS, p. 51; © Mike King/CORBIS, p. 71 (left); © Bill Hauser, p. 68; © Reuters NewMedia Inc./CORBIS, p. 71 (right).

CONTENTS

Chapter 1

HOW THIS SPORT GOT STARTED

Highest. Farthest. Longest. These three things interest athletes taking part in field events. Who can jump or **vault** the highest? Who can push a **shot** the farthest? Who can make the longest leap? While runners around the **track** take their marks and race for the fastest times, competitors inside the **oval** step up one at a time to try for their best heights and distances.

Many field events can trace their history back to the Olympic Games held in ancient Greece in 776 B.C. The first Olympics had only foot races, but later events such as the javelin, the long jump, and the **discus** were added. From the statues and the artwork on pottery that have survived

The Tailteann Games of Ireland (shown left in Dublin, 1922) were held a thousand years before the ancient Olympic Games.

THE EVENTS

Field events are divided into two categories: jumping and throwing. The jumping events include the high jump, the long jump, the triple jump, and the pole vault. The throwing events are the shot **put**, the discus throw, the hammer throw, and the javelin.

from ancient times, we can see how these events have changed. For example, long jumpers once used handheld weights during competition. They swung the weights forward on their takeoff to give them added **momentum**. On the landing, the jumpers swung the weights back to keep from falling.

Another country that contributed to modern field events was Ireland. Some historians trace back the shot put, the hammer throw, the high jump, and the pole vault to the Irish Tailteann Games, which began as long ago as the nineteenth century B.C.

Other historians date "putting the stone" to the Scottish Highland Games of the fourteenth century A.D. At these games, the participants ran up to a line before pushing the stone away from their bodies and into the air.

The high jump came down through history as a spectacle rather than as a sport. Traveling acrobats jumped over walls and the heads of their partners. It was not until 1864—at a track meet

An athlete puts a shot in the Scottish Highland Games.

between England's Oxford and Cambridge Universities—that the high jump became an organized sport.

Around that same time, the pole vault changed from being a jump for distance to a vault for height. Like the high jump, the pole vault did not start out as a sport. For centuries Europeans used pole vaulting to get over streams, canals, and marshy areas without getting their feet wet.

When the first modern Olympic Games were held in Athens, Greece, in 1896, officials selected the high jump, the long jump, the triple jump, the pole vault, the discus throw, and the shot put to be the field events. The hammer throw was added to the Paris games of 1900, and the javelin throw came on board at the 1908 London games.

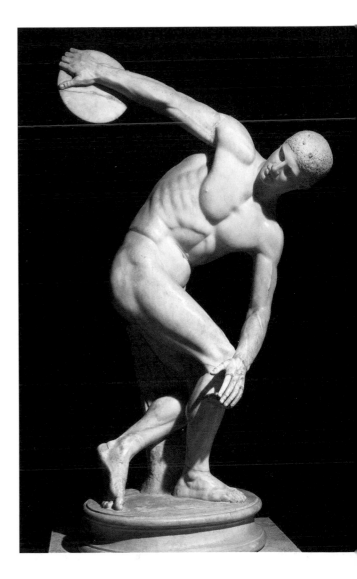

Modern discus throwers will recognize the form shown in Discobolus, *the famous bronze statue made by the sculptor Myron in 450 B.C. (A marble copy is at right.)* Discobolus *means "discus thrower" in Greek.*

WOMEN STEP UP

Women were not allowed to participate in Olympic field events until 1928, when the high jump and the discus were opened to them. At the next games, officials added the javelin. Because the Olympic Games were not held during World War II (1939–1945), women did not participate in the long jump and shot put until 1948. The hammer throw and pole vault were among the last events opened to women at the Sydney Games in 2000.

Babe Didrikson Zaharias (above) was perhaps the greatest female athlete ever. She excelled in track and field, golf, basketball, baseball, billiards, tennis, diving, and swimming. In the 1932 Olympics in Los Angeles, she won gold medals in the javelin and in the 80-meter hurdles. She also took home a silver medal in the high jump. After her success in track and field, Babe went on to become a professional golfer.

Jackie Joyner-Kersee (right) is one of the greatest heptathletes in the world. Her five Olympic medals include gold and bronze medals for the long jump.

Because the physical demands of each field event are so different, most athletes focus their efforts on one or two events. A small group of athletes will run, jump, throw, and put their way into many events. The decathlon is a two-day meet in which male athletes take part in four races and six field events. Female athletes compete in the heptathlon, which includes three track events and four field events. Athletes in both the heptathlon and decathlon receive points for their times, heights, and distances. The person with the highest point total wins. The Olympic gold medalists in each event are recognized as the best all-around athletes in the world.

In the years since the 1896 Athens games, field athletes have taken the Olympic motto of "faster, higher, stronger" to heart. Men's world records in the field events have increased by more than 20 inches in the high jump, 9 feet in the long jump, 10 feet in the pole vault, 15 feet in the triple jump, 39 feet in the shot put, and an astonishing 140 feet in the discus. Top high school athletes regularly compete at levels that would have made them the men's and women's world champions in the mid-1900s.

Improvements in technique, training, diet, and equipment allowed each generation of athletes to set new world records. By the beginning of the twenty-first century, however, the appearance of new records had slowed considerably. Have the best athletes come up against the outer limits of human ability? Only time will tell.

Chapter 2

GETTING STARTED

Each field event has its own physical requirements. For example, shot putters need power, long jumpers require speed, and pole vaulters have to have agility. All field event athletes, however, need to work on strength, endurance, and flexibility. Strong muscles allow athletes to propel themselves or objects higher and farther. Endurance ensures that athletes put as much power into their last attempt as they do into their first. And flexibility minimizes soreness and prevents injuries.

Dynamic movement, such as sprinting, helps prepare your muscles for an event.

SELECTING SHOES

There are many kinds of shoes, so be careful to choose the right pair for you. Some specialty shops sell shoes that are designed for the high jump and the discus. These shoes are for more advanced athletes. Beginners should purchase a good training shoe instead. Try on many different pairs because some manufacturers' sizes run narrow, while others run wide. Look for a pair that fits the size and shape of your foot and gives you adequate arch support.

Consider going to a shop that specializes in running shoes. Often the people who own and work in these shops are track and field fanatics. They may encourage you to take a pair of shoes for a spin outside so they can watch your technique. Their recommendations will be based on your foot shape, running style, events, and price limitations.

DEVELOPING SPEED AND ENDURANCE

Before attempting to sail over a bar or throw a discus, field athletes begin their practices with running. Not only does running warm up the body, it also increases an athlete's speed and endurance, two important things for field events. There are several different types of running used for training.

Many coaches like their athletes to begin and end practice by taking a couple of slow laps around the field. The running of these laps is called **preparation** or **recuperation jogging**. Preparation and recuperation jogging serve as both a warm-up and a cooldown because jogging stimulates blood flow to the muscles.

Another type of warm-up running is the **wind sprint**. The athlete runs at a top speed for a short distance, walks back to the **starting line**, and then runs again. Wind sprints are usually done at the beginning of practice when an athlete is fresh. Sprints are also done right before an event. This is important training because all field athletes need to produce short bursts of intense energy in their events.

Interval training requires an athlete to run at a comfortable but challenging speed for a specific amount of time. For example, an athlete will run hard for thirty seconds and then run at a slower speed for thirty seconds. The slower pace allows an athlete to recover and lower the heart rate.

Never drop down to a walk in interval training, however.

Fartlek is a Swedish word meaning "speed play." This type of running can be done anywhere, not just on the track. It's similar to interval training, except that an athlete can choose how far and long to run. The decision to speed up or slow down is made by paying attention to one's breathing and pulse. The recovery running pace should bring the heart rate back down to a near resting state.

STRETCHING FOR FLEXIBILITY

Stretching is another essential part of the warm-up and cooldown that begin and end each practice. You should spend ten to fifteen minutes stretching before practice and ten to fifteen minutes stretching afterward. Walk or jog a lap or two before stretching to increase blood flow to the muscles. While stretching, it is important to stay within your limits. Stretch slowly and easily, work both sides of the body equally, and breathe normally.

At practice, you may warm up as a team. But at meets, each athlete is responsible for his or her own stretching exercises.

Erin begins stretching her neck muscles and works her way down to her calves. She slowly tilts her head from side to side to stretch her neck.

Then she slowly brings her chin to her chest so that she feels the muscles in the back of her neck lengthen. Next, she moves on to shoulder rolls. She raises her shoulders and then rotates them back and down. After repeating this motion several times, Erin swings her arms around in wide circles.

Erin sits down to stretch her hamstring. She extends one leg and tucks the other one in. Slowly, she leans over her outstretched leg and holds the position. Erin concentrates on breathing normally during the stretch.

After holding the position for twenty to thirty seconds, she comes back up for a moment and then leans down again to deepen the stretch. She switches legs and repeats the stretch.

To stretch the quadriceps, the muscle at the front of the thigh, Rachel stands on her right leg. She lifts her left foot with her left hand so that her calf presses against the back of her thigh. She is careful to avoid injury when stretching the quadriceps.

There are many ways to stretch the calf muscles. Nikki stands an arm's length away from a wall and pushes against it with her palms. She bends her right knee and sends the left leg back so that it makes a straight line with the rest of her body. She slowly presses her left heel into the ground and feels a good stretch in the back of her left calf. She repeats the process with the other leg.

OTHER TYPES OF TRAINING

All field event athletes need to work on different muscle groups for their individual events. Strength training helps athletes build specific muscles and increase power and endurance. For example, strong abdominal muscles help long jumpers keep their feet from touching the ground too early on the landing. And upper body strength helps vaulters do almost a handstand on the pole to get over the bar. Do exercises such as sit-ups to strengthen the core muscles in your abdomen and lower back. Two other excellent forms of strength training are hill running and **weight training**.

Hill running combines strength and endurance training. Try running up the steepest hill in the neighborhood. It won't take long before your legs ache and your breathing gets harder. Your calf muscles may protest the hard work, but they'll get stronger with practice. If you train in a flat area, running up and down the bleachers is a good way to duplicate this effect. Come back down slowly, though, or you could risk damaging your knees.

Weight training is one of the best ways to build and tone muscles, but it should only be done under proper supervision with a coach or trainer. Build slowly to prevent injury. Your coach will tell you which muscles to work on, which techniques to use, and how many repetitions to attempt.

All field events are hard on the body, so it's important to give your muscles a chance to recover in order to avoid injuries. At the beginning of the season, you typically won't work on technique more than three times a week. When meets start, technique training will likely occur only twice a week.

Coaches will try to work with each athlete individually on training and technique. But coaches can't be everywhere, so athletes often work together in groups of two or three. Group members watch each other carefully, looking for breaks in form to help each other improve. Teammates also take turns raking the sandpit between jumps, raising the bar, or measuring jumps and throws. Although each athlete performs individually, practice is truly a team effort.

Chapter 3

THE LONG JUMP

In the long jump, athletes take turns sprinting down a **runway**, leaping through the air, and landing in a **pit** of sand. Their goal is to put as much distance as possible between the edge of the **takeoff board**—from which all jumps are measured—and their landings.

Depending on the rules of the meet, each athlete gets three to six attempts to jump the farthest. In some large meets, there will be a preliminary set of three jumps followed by a finals round. Only the top jumpers will move on to the finals.

A jump will not be counted if the jumper's shoe touches the ground beyond the edge of the takeoff board or **foul line**. If the shoe does cross the foul line, the athlete has **scratched**,

Sometimes the takeoff board, from which a jump is launched, is only a white stripe across the runway.

and that jump does not count. It's not against the rules, however, for jumpers to fall backward or to put their hands down in the sand upon landing. But the resulting jump will be measured from that mark instead of where the feet hit, so jumpers always try to fall forward on their landings.

The long jump is hard on the legs, so athletes typically only practice jumping two or three times a week for a short amount of time. Athletes train with two or three other teammates. They take turns jumping, measuring, and watching the takeoff board in case of a scratch. They also do leg raises and squats to build up abdominal, thigh, and hamstring muscles used for leaping and landing. Long jumpers often train with sprinters on their team to increase their speed and endurance.

A DOUBLE THREAT

The long jump is a good event for sprinters. Jesse Owens and Carl Lewis, (above) two of the greatest sprinters of the twentieth century, were also two of the best long jumpers.

Warm up for the long jump as if you were running sprints. And never let your body cool down during competition.

THE APPROACH

The **approach** to the long jump is critical. You need to hit the takeoff board—without stepping over it—just as you reach your highest speed. Consistency is essential. You should always take the same number of steps while keeping the length of your stride the same. Practice will help you make each approach nearly identical.

To choose the best point on the runway to begin your approach, start with your heel on the takeoff board and run away from the pit. Have a friend help you set **check marks**. These are spots marked on the runway to help you know where to begin your approach. Your friend should watch to see when you reach your top speed. Then he or she should mark the spot on the runway where your takeoff foot strikes the pavement. Figuring out where this happens could take a few tries. Begin your approach from that point.

Next, your friend should watch to see where your foot lands on the takeoff board during your actual jump. If your foot crosses the foul line, you should start your approach farther back. But if you are taking off long before the takeoff board, you should move up your approach. Inches count in this event, so you want to get as close to the foul line as possible without going over it. Keep in mind that the wind will also affect your approach.

Mark the runway with check marks, so you know where to begin your approach.

When you finally figure out your approach distance, measure it so you can mark your approach on the runway for future practices and meets. As you get stronger and faster through- out the season, you should make minor adjustments to your approach. You can work on these changes by running through your jump and into the sand pit during practices.

Speed is one of the keys to the long jump. The faster an athlete sprints down the runway, the more momentum his or her body will have in the air. Turning that speed into distance, however, takes technique, practice, and strength.

GOOD ADVICE

When Germany hosted the 1936 Olympics in Berlin, the leaders of the country's Nazi Party intended to display the talents of their white athletes. What they didn't plan on was Jesse Owens (above), an African American athlete. Owens came to the Berlin games and demonstrated his amazing athletic ability in track and field. His performance defied Nazi notions of the inferiority of blacks.

Owens held the world record in the long jump and considered it his best event. During the qualifying rounds, however, he found himself one jump from not making the finals. German officials had counted a warm-up jump as one of his three attempts. Then Owens scratched on his second attempt.

At that point, a German long jumper named Luz Long introduced himself to Owens. The pair talked together for a few minutes, and Long made it very clear he supported Owens.

Long suggested that Owens add a foot to his approach so that he could qualify safely and easily.

Owens took Long's advice. Both athletes advanced, and the two of them competed for the gold medal. Long equaled Owens's best distance on his fifth jump, but this only inspired Owens to add another 7 inches to his jump. When Owens clinched his gold medal with a jump of more than 26 feet, Long was the first to congratulate him.

Thirty-two years later, another American long jumper, Bob Beamon, was only one jump from missing the finals in the 1968 Olympics. Ralph Boston, another generous competitor, reminded Beamon of Long's legendary advice. Accordingly, Beamon moved his approach back in order to qualify. The next day, he set a world record of 29 feet 2½ inches, a record that stood until 1991.

THE TAKEOFF, FLIGHT, AND LANDING

There are many styles of flight in the air. They include the sit-in-the-air technique, the hang style, and the hitch-kick. They are all meant to keep the jumper in the air longer than a regular jump.

Beginners often use the sit-in-the-air technique. Athletes swing both arms forward on the takeoff and tuck their knees up to keep their feet out of the sand longer.

Most athletes prefer the hang and hitch-kick styles over the sit-in-the-air technique. Beginners use the hang style, while advanced high school and college athletes use the hitch-kick.

Nikki demonstrates the hang style. She sprints down the runway with an erect head and body. She fixes her eyes on the takeoff board until she

knows she is going to hit it. During her final few strides, she focuses her eyes on a point beyond the pit and thinks about her takeoff.

When her foot hits the takeoff board, she rocks forward off her heel and onto her toes. Her **lead leg** drives into the air for added momentum. Both of her arms go back as the lead leg drops and the takeoff leg swings forward to meet it. She seems to hang in the air for a moment with her knees bent and chest extended. To prepare for the landing, she lifts and straightens her legs. Her arms and upper body come forward.

As her heels hit the sand, she bends her knees and swings her arms back so that she pitches forward onto the sand. She breaks her fall with her hands. Her jump will be measured from the mark made by her heels in the sand because that's the closest mark to the takeoff board.

Pat is using the hitch-kick technique—the most difficult style to do. When his foot hits the takeoff board, he rocks forward onto his toes and runs off the board. He drives his lead leg high into the air and swings the arm opposite his lead leg forward, as if he's running through the air. Then his takeoff leg goes forward, while the lead leg comes back. Finally, the lead leg goes forward again for the landing. The additional steps in the air prepare him for landing.

Before landing, Pat bends forward at the waist and stretches his arms forward. As his heels come in contact

WALK THIS WAY

Always walk out of the sand pit from the end that's in front of you. Leaving from another side or end could cost you your jump or shorten your distance.

with the sand, Pat swings his arms back. This action forces his head and shoulders forward. He falls forward and puts down his hands to keep from falling face first into the sand. His jump will be measured from his closest heel mark in the sand to the takeoff board.

Chapter 4

THE TRIPLE JUMP

The triple jump is more difficult to master than the long jump is because of its three parts: the hop, the step, and the jump. The movement of the triple jump is so rhythmic that some jumpers like to envision themselves skimming across the runway in the same way that rocks skip across a pond.

Accomplished triple jumpers spend roughly the same amount of time in the air during each section. In a blur of motion, they push off the takeoff board with one foot for the hop. They land on the runway with that same foot. Then they thrust off the initial takeoff foot for the step, but this time

EQUIPMENT

Beginning triple jumpers should always wear heel guards to prevent injuries. Some beginners also wear hurdling shoes with spikes.

they land on the other foot. Finally, they leap into the air and land in the pit with both feet to complete the jump. The trailing leg cannot touch the runway at any point during the hop, step, or jump. If it does, the athlete has **fouled**, or scratched.

Because the triple jump is even harder on the legs than the long jump, triple jumpers rarely practice full jumps. They give special attention to the hop and step portions instead. Athletes also practice one-legged hops, alternate **leg bounds**, uphill bounds, and hurdles. Triple jumpers spend the rest of their practice time working out with the sprinters and building up lower body strength.

GETTING STARTED

It's important to master the basic footwork before attempting a running approach. Go work in an open field. Once there, figure out which leg you will use to begin the hop. This initial takeoff leg should be your strongest leg since it will be used twice. Start from a standing position. Hop forward on your takeoff foot. Land on that same foot and swing your other leg forward with power for a giant step. Land flat-footed. Finally, push off for the jump and land on both feet. As you become comfortable, pick a mark on the grass and add a few approach steps. Begin at a walk, move on to a trot, and gradually work up to the fastest approach you can master while still using good technique.

You are ready for the runway. Just like in the long jump, it's important to set check marks for the triple jump. Begin at the takeoff board and have a teammate watch to see at what point you reach your fastest speed. You will want to put your check mark there when you can perform the triple jump at top speed. As you learn control and technique for this difficult jump, you can make gradual adjustments to your speed and starting point.

PAWING ACTION

Triple jumpers describe the way their foot hits the ground during the hop, the step, and the jump as a pawing action. Don't let your heel hit the ground first, or you risk injury.

THE HOP, STEP, JUMP, AND LANDING

Pat sprints down the runway with his knees high. He has been working to use the same number of steps in his approach. He focuses his eyes on the takeoff board for part of the approach but looks ahead as he begins the hop.

Pat plants his foot for the hop as he reaches the takeoff board. He drives the knee of his lead leg forward so that his thigh is parallel to the ground. But Pat does not go for height

4

5

6

when leaving the takeoff board. He takes off at an angle of only 15 to 18 degrees. His takeoff leg swings forward and then back, ready to land and push off again. He positions his leg so that he will land on his entire foot for the step. During the hop, Pat coordinates his arms with his legs. When his right leg swings forward, so does his left arm.

For the step, Pat drives with his initial takeoff leg and steps up and forward with his lead leg. His head is high, his body upright. He swings his arms to add momentum and to keep his body balanced. He lands on his lead leg and prepares for the jump.

During the jump, Pat will try for height as well as distance. This can be tough because he will be pushing off with his weaker leg. Pat drives both his arms forward. His takeoff leg swings forward until it is even with his lead leg. Pat begins to straighten both legs as he bends his body forward for the landing.

To land, Pat swings both of his arms down and back so that his head and shoulders go forward over his legs. He bends his knees as he lands so his body will pitch forward into the sand. The length of his jump will be measured from the foul line to his first mark in the sand.

7

8

9

10

Chapter 5

THE HIGH JUMP

The high jump is one of the most amazing events to watch. In high-level competition, jumpers soar more than 12 inches above the top of their own heads. When you're just starting out, you won't be able to duplicate such feats, but you will experience the feel of flight as you sail over the **crossbar**. As your strength and technique improve, you might find yourself looking up at the bar, amazed at the height you've **cleared.**

BASIC EQUIPMENT

In the high jump, a bar is placed at varying heights on top of two metal poles. A large, soft foam mat lies behind the poles.

The goal of the high jump is simple: to get your body over the bar, or clear the bar, without knocking it down. You can take as many approaches as are needed—within a certain time limit—as long as no part of your body touches the bar. You have three chances to clear a height. You may pass on a height, but you only get credit for the last height cleared. Three failed jumps in a row disqualify you from the competition. The win goes to the jumper with the fewest misses, or scratches.

OTHER SPORTS

Some athletes play other sports to train for field events. For example, playing volleyball or basketball will strengthen your legs for the jumping and pivoting done in the high jump.

High jumpers should spend time improving flexibility, strength, and technique. Lift weights to help build strong abdominal muscles for kicking your legs over the bar right before landing. Don't practice jumping more than three times a week, however.

Spend the rest of your practice working on speed and endurance with the sprinters. Speed is important because the faster you are, the more momentum you can transfer into sailing over the bar. Endurance is critical so that your legs don't start to feel heavy as you move onto the higher heights.

THE FIRST APPROACH

A beginning high jumper might be intimidated by the sight of an experienced teammate sailing over the bar with seemingly little effort. The key to reaching that level of skill is to take it one step at a time.

The first thing a beginning high jumper should do is to select a takeoff leg and foot. Generally, left-handed people prefer to spring off their right foot while right-handed people prefer to use their left foot. You may want to experiment by jumping over a few hurdles. Whichever leg feels the most comfortable and strongest to spring off of should be your takeoff leg.

Many coaches encourage beginners to start with the **scissors kick**. This style isn't used in competition anymore, but it helps beginners learn the fundamentals of the high jump while learning to land on the mat properly.

To try the scissors kick, set the bar at a low height and then stand an arm's length away from it. Drive your inside leg up and throw your arms into the air. Next, bring up your outside, or **plant leg,** in a scissors action until you are almost sitting above the bar. You will land on the mat.

Once the basic motion of the scissors kick is achieved, you can add steps to your approach. Try the first three steps slowly, beginning with your strongest foot. Lengthen your stride with the next four steps. Plant your strong foot, or takeoff foot, when you are an arm's length from the bar. Repeat the scissors motion.

THE FOSBURY FLOP

The Fosbury Flop is the easiest style of high jumping to learn as well as the most effective. It was named for Dick Fosbury, who introduced his revolutionary technique to the world at the 1968 Olympics in Mexico City. The crowd was stunned and delighted when Fosbury pivoted

IN STYLE WITH THE TIMES

Since the introduction of the high jump to intercollegiate competition in 1864, the sport has undergone many changes in style. The scissors kick, straddle, and Western roll all had several decades of popularity. When performed properly, each ensured that the athlete landed safely in pits filled with sand and sawdust. The introduction of the deep foam mat allowed American Dick Fosbury to create his revolutionary flop that changed high jumping forever.

on his takeoff foot, turned his back to the mat, and sailed over the bar headfirst.

One of the keys to a good jump is setting up the approach. For the Fosbury Flop, the approach path looks like the letter J, with the hook occurring as you approach the bar. Most right-handed people feel comfortable approaching the high jump from the right.

Rachel begins with one foot on her check mark and the other behind it. Her first few strides are slow and springy. Her next few strides are faster and longer. As she begins the curve of the J, she leans away from the bar. Rachel's strides become shorter and quicker as she runs on her entire foot and not just on the balls of her feet.

Rachel **plants** her outside foot, the one farthest away from the bar, and drives her arms and inside leg into the air. She pivots on her planted foot so that her back is to the bar. As Rachel takes off, she continues to turn in the air while leaning back with her upper body. She tucks her chin in and turns her head to look over the bar. Her hands remain up until she clears the bar. She snaps her head back and then

1

2

It is against the rules to take off with two feet in the high jump. Until 1936, the rules also stated that the jumper had to jump feet first.

pulls her legs over, careful to keep her heels away from the bar. She spreads her arms out to cushion the blow on her shoulders and arms. Since Rachel has cleared the bar, her jump will count, and she will move on to the next height.

ADJUSTING YOUR APPROACH

As your strength, conditioning, and technique improve, you may have to make small adjustments to the approach. If you frequently hit the bar with your shoulders on the way up or down on low heights, you're too close to the bar. To work on the approach, stand an arm's length away from the center of the bar. Push off your takeoff foot. Keeping a careful count of your springing steps, trace the curve of the J back to what would be your normal starting point. Many athletes use this technique to set up their check mark at the meet.

Chapter 6

THE POLE VAULT

Some people call the pole vault gymnastics on a stick. Great pole vaulters make the event look like one smooth, continuous motion. They use a long pole to catapult their bodies through the air and over a crossbar at amazing heights, often 3 feet over their pole **grip**.

Similar to the high jumpers, athletes in the pole vault compete until they fail to clear the bar three times in a row on a height. Vaulters often have to get through a **qualifying round** to compete in the event. After they successfully complete a vault at the qualifying height, they may pass on, or choose not to vault, successive heights. Athletes strategize about which heights to attempt and which ones to pass on. Athletes make those judgments based on their past work in the vault and their stamina. They will only receive credit for the heights that they have successfully cleared. The win will go to the athlete with the fewest misses.

SERGEI BUBKA

Sergei Bubka began his dominance in the pole vault in 1983. Entire stadiums would grow quiet as he attacked the bar. As time went on, it became clear that his only competition was himself. But even the man who set more than eighteen indoor and seventeen outdoor world records could have a bad meet. In the 1992 Olympics in Barcelona, Bubka stepped up for his opening vault and did the unthinkable. He missed. He also failed at his next two attempts and wound up finishing dead last. Some writers declared his career over, but Bubka persevered and went on to set new records.

THE POLE

The pole vault is the only field event that requires a tool to enhance the athlete's performance. The first poles were made of ash or hickory with a piece of iron on the end to keep the pole from sliding. Eventually, a wooden **vaulting box** was introduced so vaulters could attack the bar at full speed.

The introduction of the flexible fiberglass pole caused another change in technique. Instead of swinging up to the bar on the pole in a smooth arc, athletes deliberately bend the flexible fiberglass pole at the beginning of the vault. That way the pole can propel them at the top of the vault. This innovation in technique allowed the winning Olympic height to shoot up an additional 3 feet over the course of twelve years.

Every pole is marked with its length and its **weight rating**. The pole's weight rating sets the maximum number of pounds an athlete can weigh and still safely use a given pole. In international competition, male athletes use 17-foot poles. Beginners should start with a much shorter pole of 10 to 12 feet. You should *never* vault with a pole if you are heavier than its weight rating.

Most coaches teach the basics of pole vaulting by starting off an athlete on a rigid pole with a weight rating that greatly exceeds his or her weight. Beginners will soon achieve heights greater than the distance of a foot above their outstretched hand to the ground. Vaulters can then begin working on the complicated task of bending the pole while still maintaining forward momentum.

If you are left-handed, carry your pole on the left side with your right hand forward.

PREPARING TO VAULT

Pat grips the pole loosely. Since he is right-handed, he carries the pole on his right side. His right hand is to the back of the pole with the palm facing up. His left hand is forward with the palm facing down. The spacing between the hands varies from athlete to athlete, depending on what is comfortable, but it is usually a little wider than shoulder width.

1

2

Pat points his pole straight down the runway. His shoulders stay square to the bar. The end of his pole slants up into the air.

Pat stands at his check mark on the runway so that he will reach his top speed a few strides before he plants his pole. He knows that the faster his speed is while still maintaining control, the higher he'll be able to vault.

Pat begins his approach with long, slow strides. He accelerates smoothly. He runs on his toes with his knees high. Gradually, the tip of his pole comes down.

A few strides ahead of the box, Pat moves the pole slightly forward. His right hand is close to his hip. He fights the natural inclination to slow down as he prepares to plant his pole into the vaulting box.

3

4

THE VAULT

Pat puts the end of the pole into the middle of the box. This crucial step is the plant. He drives his right knee up and forward almost in the same way that a long jumper launches into the air. He lengthens his body and tries to keep his trailing leg straight. His arms are extended, pushing on the pole.

Two strides before his takeoff, Pat prepares for the next step by raising his right hand to bring the front of the pole down. He fully extends his arms so that his hands and the back of the pole pass above his head.

Pat rocks back and bends the pole. This will give him more momentum to get over the bar. His knees and hips travel up above his shoulders as his left arm begins to bend at the elbow. He keeps his head in line with his body.

Pat continues to rock back until he is upside down. At that moment, he does a handstand on the pole. His arms are extended again, and his body is almost parallel with the pole. He pulls with his right hand and lets go of the pole with his left hand. His body quickly rotates a quarter turn and bends at the waist as he begins his downward descent. Then Pat pushes the pole away from the bar. He falls downward and lands on his back. Since he has successfully cleared the bar at this height, he won't jump again until the next height.

5

8

9

6

7

10

11

TRAINING

As you watch a pole vaulter charge down the runway and launch into the air, it is difficult to imagine breaking the moves down into their individual parts. But some coaches do just that when they lead their beginning vaulters over to the long jump pits.

Using this method, a coach can show athletes the evolution of the pole vault from its early beginnings as a distance event. After the grip and takeoff are mastered, you start by vaulting for distance. Once that feels comfortable, it's time to introduce some additional speed and power. Try turning your body in the air so you land facing the runway. Next, the crossbar is added. Gradually, the height of the crossbar rises. By the

end of a few hours, you can be vaulting safely and correctly. You won't be bending the pole yet, but you will have learned proper technique.

All work on the pole vault should be done under the direct supervision of a coach. Sometimes, if no one on the coaching staff has any pole vaulting experience, an expert will come in for a few hours a week.

During the rest of practice, work on increasing your speed and stamina. The faster you make the approach, the more forward momentum you can transfer into achieving height. Try

BENDING THE POLE

If you find yourself bending the pole more than 90 degrees, change to a stiffer pole. If one isn't available, move your grip lower on the pole during your vault. Lowering your grip also prevents loss of momentum.

running hard for 40 to 220 yards and then walking. Spend time on gymnastic events, such as the rings, to increase your strength and agility.

SAFETY

Pole vaulters need to attack the bar without fear. There is, however, a difference between courage and carelessness. Common sense and the ability to concentrate are two of the main things that coaches look for in their pole vaulters. Avoid foolish mistakes that could hurt you or others.

Poles undergo enormous stress during the vault. Always inspect your pole before a meet or practice. Check for nicks and cuts in the pole. You should not lay your pole down on the ground unless it is in a carrying case.

Keep the area within a 10-foot radius of the pole vault clear of people and hard objects on which you could fall. Never grip the pole above the 6-inch safety line, or you could snap the pole. If the pole **stalls** (stops moving forward before reaching a vertical position), hang on to the pole. If you let go, you could find yourself tumbling to the ground headfirst.

In vaulting, your back is meant for landing. With the exception of a few drills, you should avoid landing on your feet. If you land on your feet, there's a good chance that you'll

HIGHER AND HIGHER

Stacy Dragila picked up her first vaulting pole in 1993, before the pole vault was recognized as an official event for women. "The first couple trillion times going over the bar were pretty frightening for me," she has admitted. But no one who watched her three-hour battle for the gold medal in the 2000 Olympic Games in Sydney would have guessed. Dragila beat Australia's Tatiana Grigorieva and Iceland's Vala Flosadottir and won the gold with a vault of 15 feet 1 inch. As women continue to develop their speed and technique in the pole vault, Dragila believes that heights of 17 feet will become possible.

bounce off the mat and land on your head.

Finally, always wear a helmet. Wearing a helmet is important because most serious injuries occur when a vaulter falls off the mat. After a few days use, you won't even realize that you're wearing one.

Chapter 7

THE SHOT PUT

An athlete enters the **throwing circle**. The spectators remain quiet as a shot sails into the air. The shot's thud is greeted with applause. Although this scene sounds like it's from a golf tournament, it's actually the shot put—one of the many throwing competitions in field events.

People unfamiliar with the shot put often think the athlete *throws* a heavy ball, or shot, down the field, but the actual motion is a push called a put. The athlete gets three attempts to put the shot from a circle on the field. If the competitor steps on or past the **toe board**, it is a foul, and that attempt will neither be measured nor counted. Once the shot strikes the ground, the athlete can leave the circle.

HEADS UP

Even though the shot put is considered the safest of all weight-throwing events, extreme care must still be exercised. It's dangerous to have 4-, 6-, and 8-pound metal spheres flying through the air. Other events such as the hammer throw and the discus are not even introduced until high school or college and then only under the close supervision of a coach.

PUT YOUR BODY INTO IT

In the throwing events, athletes tend to be solidly built instead of lean and fast. But strength, size, and speed are not enough. It takes technique to transfer the most force from your body to the shot put. The pushing arm needs power and speed, but the whole body must be used in putting the shot. Some coaches will chant "Legs, legs, legs, legs!" at members of their team to remind them of the power in their thighs.

Judges measure a shot's distance from the point where the shot first hits the ground within the **throwing sector**. The throwing sector allows the judges to get close enough to judge the put with reasonable accuracy. Measuring accurately is easier at outdoor meets, because the shot will often leave a small dent in the ground where it lands.

Athletes practice putting the shot two or three times a week. They continue to practice the basic put even after mastering a more advanced technique. They prepare for tough training sessions by doing wind sprints and endurance running. To increase strength in the arms and legs, shot putters have their coach guide them through a weight-training program.

The Throwing Circle

THE GRIP

The athlete grips the shot in preparation for his turn. Most people prefer to push the shot with their writing hand. This athlete is right-handed, so he uses his left hand to position the shot on the palm of his right hand. He supports most of the ball's weight on the base of his three middle fingers. He spreads his fingers around the ball to balance it in his hand. His thumb wraps around the ball on the inside.

He places the shot against his neck, resting it directly under his ear and jaw. His elbow is out at shoulder height. He relaxes his wrist so that his hand supports the weight of the shot.

1

THE STANDING PUT

An experienced shot putter will glide, hop, or spin across the circle with agility and a certain grace. But beginners should first learn the standing position. The standing put strengthens muscles and helps to coordinate arm and leg motions.

Brie presses the outside of her left foot against the toe board. She places her right foot in a direct line between her left foot and the center of the circle. As Brie bends and twists at the waist, she rests most of her weight on her right, or inside, foot.

2

3

4

5

In an explosive motion, Brie pushes the shot up and out and pivots off her right foot. At the same time, her left arm leads her body while she turns and straightens. As her weight shifts to her front foot, she drives her right arm up so that her elbow remains behind her wrist. Her arm makes a 45-degree angle to the ground.

Once the shot leaves Brie's hand, she hops off her left foot and comes down on her right foot. Her left leg stays extended in the air to provide balance. This move helps keep Brie behind the toe board.

6

DRIVING ACROSS THE CIRCLE

After you master the motions of the standing put, it's time to learn how to drive, or glide, across the circle. You should continue to practice the standing put, even after mastering the glide. The added momentum gained by the glide, however, will add power and distance to your throws. You will finish the glide with the motions of the standing put.

Megan begins at the back of the circle. Since she is right-handed, she points her right foot toward the back of the throwing circle, 180 degrees from the direction she wants to throw. She rests the shot against her neck and leans over her bent leg. The toe of Megan's left shoe rests on the ground. The bottom of her foot is facing the direction of her throw.

Megan prepares to hop, or glide, backward by driving her left leg forward and then snapping it back toward the toe board. In a low, gliding hop, she moves her right foot to the center of the circle so that her back foot finishes

4

5

near the toe board. Megan is in a position very close to the beginning of the standing put. In a smooth motion, she straightens her right leg with force and turns her body toward the center of the toe board. She keeps her elbow behind her wrist as she powers the shot away from her body. As Megan releases the shot, her arm makes a 45-degree angle to the ground.

To keep from stepping on or over the toe board on the **follow-through**, Megan hops off her left foot and then lands on her right foot. Her left leg will end high in the air for balance. A judge will measure where Megan's shot landed and tell her how she did.

FOUL!

Bob Mathias was still in high school when his track coach encouraged him to try the decathlon. After three months of training, he earned a spot on the U.S. Olympic team for the 1948 games in London. During the shot put, Mathias managed to send the shot beyond the 45-foot marker. Satisfied with his attempt, he stepped out of the throwing circle. Suddenly, an official raised a flag signifying that he had committed a foul. He had stepped out of the front of the circle instead of the back. No one had remembered to tell Mathias the rule. Despite the foul, he placed high in the shot put and went on to win his first of two gold medals in the decathlon.

Chapter 8

THE DISCUS

An accomplished discus thrower spins across the circle with grace and ease before launching a discus into the sky. At the higher levels of competition, the discus thrower makes a dizzying one and one-half turns while moving straight across the circle.

The technique and equipment of the discus throw are different from those of the shot put, but the basic rules of these two events are similar. Throwers get three attempts. If they step outside the throwing circle before the discus lands, the throw will be disqualified. Competitors must leave the throwing circle by the back, or they will foul.

The throwing circle in the discus throw has no toe board, but the circle is larger—8.2 feet in diameter—to allow for the spinning technique used in the discus throw. A **cage** is placed behind the throwing circle to protect the judges, spectators, and other participants from a wild throw.

THE SHOT PUT VS. DISCUS

While the technique used for the shot put is quite different from the other throwing events, the muscle strength, endurance, and discipline gained in the shot put can be transferred to the discus throw. Speed has more importance in the discus than in the shot put, however.

Distance is measured from where the discus lands inside the throwing sector, but throwers don't get to hope for a good roll. A pair of judges will stand in the throwing sector just beyond the range of the athletes participating. Their job is to get close enough to the discus to see where it lands without getting hit by it.

To train for the discus throw, work on improving speed and technique so your body is prepared to do quick, powerful movements. Practice your technique by throwing lightweight and heavyweight objects. Do sprints, overhead squats, and bench presses to develop speed, endurance, strength, and flexibility.

AN ADDITIONAL TWISTING STRETCH

The twisting and turning motions involved in slinging a discus into the sky require an additional stretch for the back and shoulder muscles. Mike stands with his feet shoulder width apart. Without moving his hips, he twists the upper half of his body so he is looking over his shoulder and down the length of his extended right arm. Then he twists his torso in the opposite direction and looks down the length of his other arm.

GETTING STARTED

The first step to throwing the discus is to choose your throwing hand. Most athletes select the hand that they write with. Arrange the discus so that the first joint of every finger overlaps the rim, and your palm and wrist press against the top of the discus. During the throw, the force generated by the swinging motion of your arm will keep the discus pressed against the palm and wrist.

Next, practice the standing throw, the most basic discus technique. Mike demonstrates. He stands with his feet on an imaginary line that would extend from the center of the circle to the center of the throwing sector. His right hand and right leg are closest to the center of the circle. As he swings the arm with the discus backward, he puts his weight on his back foot and bends at the knees. Then he brings the discus forward, shifting his weight to his front foot.

Notice the position of Mike's feet and upper body in the throwing circle as he prepares to do a standing throw. He twists the upper half of his body to face the throwing sector.

Mike's other hand comes up to shoulder level, and the discus rests momentarily on his upturned palm. Mike swings his arm back and down and then brings it up once more. On each repetition of the swivel, he bends his knees a little lower and swings his arm faster to generate momentum.

On the final swing, Mike brings the discus as far back as possible with his arm and shoulders while leaning over his bent right knee. As he brings the discus up, he pivots on his front foot. His shoulders follow the movement of his hips.

Mike releases the discus at shoulder level. His index finger is the last part of his body to touch the discus. His goal is to achieve a high, level spinning throw. After pivoting on his front foot, Mike hops onto his back foot to avoid stepping outside the throwing circle.

ADDING THE SPIN

Once you have mastered the standing throw, you can add a spin to your delivery. The spin will add momentum, but there isn't any point to the extra momentum until you can control it.

The athlete begins by facing the back of the circle. He swings the discus back and forth several times just as Mike practiced in the standing throw.

Since the thrower is right-handed, he starts his spin by pushing off of his right foot and pivoting on the left. He makes sure that the movement of the discus trails the rotation of his hips.

4

5

6

The athlete lands on the ball of his right foot and pivots on that. His left leg swings around. He plants his foot so that his toe is pointing toward the center of the throwing sector. His shoulders continue rotating until he smoothly releases the discus. He finishes by hopping off his left foot and planting the right leg to stay within the throwing circle. He watches the discus land inside the throwing sector before he leaves the circle from the back.

7

8

AL OERTER

Successful athletes know how to perform well at the big meets in their careers. Al Oerter made his first appearance in the discus at the 1956 Olympics in Melbourne, Australia, as an excited kid whose first throw of the day was enough to win him a gold medal. During the next two Olympics, he overcame injury to win two more gold medals.

When Oerter qualified for his fourth Olympics, however, he was an aging veteran. His best throw was 16 feet shorter than that of the world record holder. When the discus was delayed due to rain, several of the competitors became nervous. With more than 33,000 throws behind him, Oerter stayed calm. On his second attempt, he launched the best throw of his long career. Oerter's throw, along with the rain delay, destroyed the confidence of his opponents. Oerter went on to win his fourth gold medal.

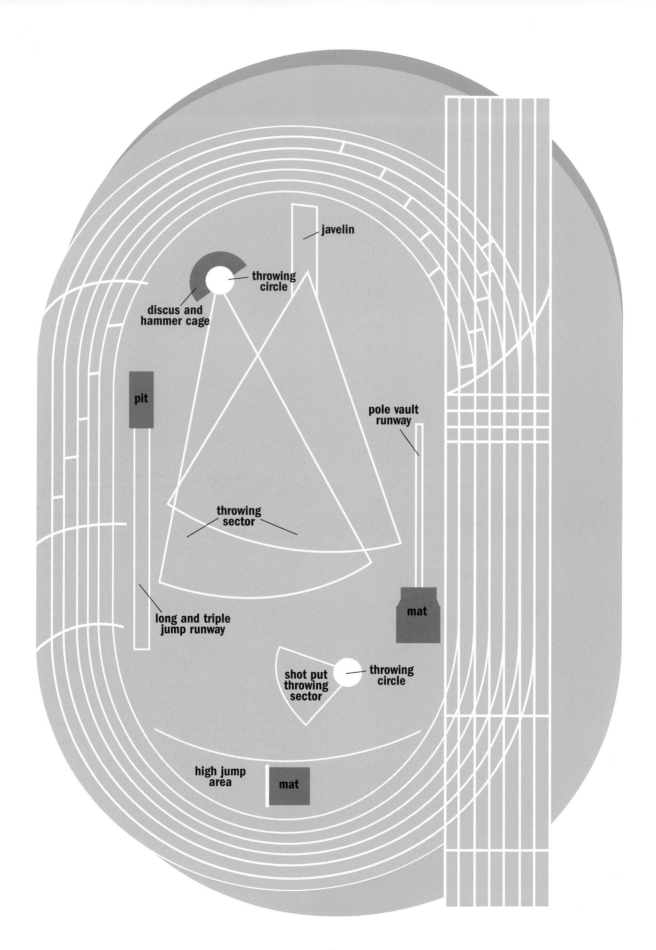

javelin

throwing circle

discus and hammer cage

pit

pole vault runway

throwing sector

long and triple jump runway

mat

shot put throwing sector

throwing circle

high jump area

mat

Chapter 9

THE MEET

After spending hours improving speed, strength, endurance, and technique, field event athletes have a chance to step forward at a meet and have their efforts officially measured by an impartial judge.

A meet can be anything from an afternoon gathering of two or three schools to a daylong event with eight or more schools participating. Even the best-planned meet will seem chaotic because many events are scheduled at the same time—both around the track and inside the oval. Loudspeakers blare out announcements. The starter's pistol cracks. Crowds cheer for the runners pounding down the straightaway. Spectators groan as a pole vaulter fails to clear the bar. Athletes jog around the track for their warm-ups. Lines form at the pit for the long jump and the triple jump.

In a meet, athletes can score points for their team by placing high in their individual events. The team with the most points wins the meet.

It is the responsibility of every athlete to get to the proper location at the proper time. Although schedules are provided to coaches, athletes, and spectators, it's important to pay attention to the first, second, and final calls issued by the loudspeaker.

Coaches and meet organizers do their best to arrange the events so that athletes participating in more than one will have a chance to rest between events. Certain allowances are always made, however. For example, long jumpers often participate in other events, such as sprints, hurdles, and the triple jump. While athletes have to check in for their first jump when their event is called, they can complete the rest of their jumps as the jumps fit into their other events. The situation for high jumpers and pole vaulters is different because of the way the bar is gradually raised. If they have to leave the area to run in a sprint or relay, they are allowed ten minutes or so to rest before making another attempt.

As much as you'd like to cheer for your teammates, it's more important for you to rest and prepare yourself mentally and physically for your own events. Don't start your personal warm-up too early. About a half an hour before your event begins, take a short jog. Spend ten minutes stretching your muscles from your neck to your calves. Keep moving even after

you have completed your warm-up. It's important to stay calm and loose when competing. You will not be able to perform as well if your muscles are tense. Don't worry that you will use up too much energy. You won't be able to use the strength and energy you have if you allow your muscles to cool down. When the air is cool, it's a good idea to put your sweats back on as you wait for your next turn. Putting on extra clothes will help

SHOWDOWN

At the 1988 Olympics in Seoul, Korea, American Louise Ritter and Stefka Kostadinova of Bulgaria left the rest of the high jumpers behind. But when the bar was set to 6 feet 8 inches, both athletes knocked it down on each of their three attempts. First place usually goes to the athlete with the fewest misses. But neither of them had missed on a single attempt at a lower height, so they went to a sudden-death jump-off. Kostadinova, who held the world record of 6 feet 10 inches, failed on her fourth attempt at 6 feet 8 inches. Ritter made it and won the gold.

keep your muscles warm.

Once you have finished your events for the day, you can watch your friends compete. Let's see what a meet would be like by following three teammates taking part in the high jump, the triple jump, and the discus throw.

LET'S COMPETE!

Dan, a high jumper, steps up to his check mark. He looks at the high jump bar, which has been adjusted to the qualifying height of 5 feet 8 inches. Then he glances over his shoulder at the track starting line. The runners have taken their marks for the 100-meter dash. Dan decides to wait until the race is finished before making his attempt.

The starter's gun fires, and the runners sprint down the straightaway. Twelve seconds later, the race is complete, and the crowd in the bleachers quiets down. Dan leans his weight on his back foot and then rocks forward. He repeats this process twice as part of his mental preparation. Then he strides forward with long, springy steps. Slowly, he accelerates, careful to keep a bounce. Dan tilts his body away

from the bar until he is parallel to it.

He launches off his left foot and drives his arm into the air, clearing the bar with inches to spare. Then Dan falls backward onto the mat.

Dan rolls off the mat and walks over to the spot where he had left his sweats. He needs to check in at the long jump pit. After that, he'll return to the high jump.

As Dan pulls on his sweats, Megan nears the front of the line at the triple jump. She jogs in place to keep her muscles warm. With only two people standing in front of her, she stops to think about her next jump. In her head, she counts her steps to the takeoff board. Then she visualizes herself skimming over the ground like a rock on a pond before launching herself into the air.

Finally, Megan's turn arrives. She steps across the starting line and uses the tape stretched out along the runway to set her check mark. She stands there a few seconds before taking her first step down the runway. She drives her arms and legs faster. As her entire foot comes down to begin the hop, only the toe of her right shoe hits the takeoff board. She sails into the air. Her right foot hits the runway again, and she launches into the step. She lands on her left foot and performs the jump. Megan brings both feet forward to prepare for her landing in the pit. She falls forward into the sand and immediately scrambles to her feet.

"Mark," the official says, and his assistant puts the tape in the sand at the nearest mark to the takeoff board.

"Thirty-three feet 11 inches," the official announces.

Megan smiles. The mark is only a few inches short of her **personal best**, and she still has one more chance to jump. But she had already heard the second call for the 800-meter run while she was standing in line. She knows that the race is right before her **heat** in the 110-meter hurdles. She will want time to prepare for both events. She will have to return and take her last jump later.

As Megan dusts the grains of sand from the pit off her hands and knees, Lana Sinykin stands behind the discus cage. She waits for the official to announce her turn.

The sand in the pit must be raked after each jump so officials can easily measure the next jump.

WHO'S UP NEXT?

At a meet, shot putters and discus throwers are often separated into **flights.** The official will read the list of athletes the same way that a baseball coach reads off a batting order. The first person is up, the second is on deck, and the third is in the hole.

"Sinykin is up, Ransom is on deck, and Kangas is in the hole."

Hearing her last name called, Lana steps into the throwing circle and faces the back of the cage. She lowers the discus onto her palm and wrist and arranges her fingertips on the rim. She swings the discus back and then up and around to rest briefly on her left palm. She repeats the movement three times, her moves gaining speed and intensity. Then in a blur of action, she steps back with her left foot and begins spinning across the circle.

The discus leaves Lana's hand and spins through the air in a flat arc. After her release, Lana hops twice as she watches the discus spin through the air. Two people carefully trot to a spot near where the discus will strike the ground. It bounces and rolls away.

"Mark," the official announces as Lana steps out of the back of the circle. One person runs to get the tape while the other stays close to where the discus struck the ground.

"Sinykin—102 feet 3 inches."

Yes! Lana smiles. Two of her teammates clap. Although the measurement is 10 feet behind where the winner's discus will probably land, it is Lana's personal best. Before her flight ends, she will have two more opportunities to step into the circle and show what she can do.

Only a fcw people will step onto the world stage and go for gold, but those who participate in field events at every level struggle to add inches and feet to their best heights and distances. These athletes compete against more than just the other athletes. They compete against themselves and for their teams.

An official marks where the discus lands.

FIELD TALK

approach: The steps taken down the runway to prepare an athlete for the long jump, the triple jump, and the pole vault

cage: A metal enclosure placed behind the discus throwing circle to protect officials, athletes, and spectators from a wild throw

check mark: A spot that pole vaulters, long jumpers, and high jumpers select on the runway to ensure that their approach is similar every time

clear: In the high jump or pole vault, to successfully make it over the crossbar without knocking it down

crossbar: A pole resting lightly on a set of uprights. The crossbar is raised to a certain height for the pole vault and high jump. Also called a bar

discus: A circular object with a wooden or plastic center and an outside rim made of metal. It is thicker in the center than on the outside rim. It weighs 2.2 pounds for high school girls, 3.52 pounds for high school boys, and 4.4 pounds for college athletes.

flight: A group of athletes that competes consecutively in the discus or shot put

follow-through: The act of continuing a motion until its natural completion after the release of the shot or discus

foul: Allowing the foot to go past the throwing circle or takeoff line. The attempt will not be measured. A foul is also called a scratch.

foul line: The edge of the takeoff board closest to the pit from which all jumps are measured. If a jumper's shoe crosses the foul line, that jump will not be measured.

grip: The way an athlete holds an object such as a vaulting pole, a shot, or a discus

interval training: Running fast for a specific amount of time and then running at a slower pace for the same amount of time

heat: A single round of a race with two or more rounds

lead leg: The leg that swings into the air on a jump while the other leg is pushing off the ground

leg bound: A long bouncing stride where the athlete drives his or her knees high into the air

momentum: The force or speed an object has when it is moving. In general, the greater an object's momentum, the farther it will travel before coming to a stop.

oval: The oval-shaped racetrack that surrounds the area where field events take place

personal best: An individual's top officially measured height or distance

pit: The sandy area where triple jumpers and long jumpers land. It is used to make measurements easier and to minimize the impact of a landing on a jumper's legs.

plant: To place, or put, one's leg in a position on the ground to prepare for a jump. Also, to place the end of a vaulting pole into the vaulting box

plant leg: The leg with which the athlete jumps in the high jump

preparation jogging: Slow laps used to prepare an athlete's muscles for physical activity. Jogging stimulates blood flow to the muscles.

put: The act of launching the shot up and away from the body

qualifying round: A jump or vault at specific height that each athlete must complete successfully before continuing in the competition

recuperation jogging: Slow laps used to cool down an athlete's muscles after physical activity

runway: The narrow strip of track, measuring 150 feet in length, between the starting line and takeoff board. It is used as the approach for the long jump, the triple jump, and the pole vault.

scissors kick: A style of high jumping where the legs move like scissors as they cross over the bar

scratch: To have a jump, vault, or throw disqualified

shot: A spherical metal ball weighing between 6.61 pounds for the youngest competitors to 16 pounds for male collegiate and international competitors. High school athletes use either 8.81-pound or 12-pound balls. The first shots ever put were probably leftover ammunition from light cannons.

stall: When a vault loses forward momentum before reaching a vertical position. A stalled pole vaulter will not make it to the mat.

starting line: A line on the runway that athletes must stand behind for their turn

takeoff board: A board on the runway that is level with the track and will not move. The board is 8 to 24 inches wide and 4 feet long. Sometimes a white stripe is painted on the runway instead.

throwing circle: A circle 8 feet 2½ inches in diameter. An athlete must remain in the circle while putting the shot or throwing the discus. The distance of a throw is measured from its landing point to the edge of the circle.

78

throwing sector: A 40- to 60-degree arc measured from the center of the throwing circle. Only shots that land within the throwing sector count as a legal throw.

toe board: A 4-inch-high board with a curved length of 4 feet. It is set firmly into the ground on the front edge of the throwing circle for the shot put. Some shot putters use the board to stop their forward momentum.

track: An oval with eight lanes used for running races

vault: To propel oneself over a crossbar using a pole

vaulting box: An aluminum, steel, or fiberglass box where pole vaulters plant their poles at the takeoff. The box measures 3 feet in length and 60 centimeters in width. Its top is even with the runway and slopes down to a depth of 20 centimeters below the runway. The inside of the box is 60 centimeters at the runway and 15 centimeters near the pit.

weight rating: A number on each pole that sets the maximum number of pounds an athlete can weigh and still use that pole

weight training: Supervised use of free weights and weight machines to increase strength

wind sprint: A type of running done at a top speed for a short distance. It is used to develop an athlete's breathing capacity.

FURTHER READING

Jackson, Colin. *The Young Track and Field Athlete.* New York: Dorling Kindersley Limited, 1996.

Wallenchinsky, David. *The Complete Book of the Olympics.* New York: Viking Press, 1984.

FOR MORE INFORMATION

International Amateur Athletics Federation (IAAF)
17 rue Princesse Florestine
BP 359
MC 98007 Monaco
www.iaaf.org

National Federation of State High School Associations (NFHS)
11724 NW Plaza Circle
P.O. Box 20626
Kansas City, MO 64195
www.nfhs.org

U.S.A. Track and Field (USATF)
One RCA Dome, Suite 140
Indianapolis, IN 46225
www.usatf.org

INDEX

ABOUT THE AUTHOR

Kristin Wolden Nitz is a substitute teacher and children's author. Her best field event used to be the high jump. She holds a degree in electrical engineering from Michigan Technological University. Since graduating from college, she has lived in Connecticut, Florida, New York, Washington, Nebraska, and Italy. She lives in Missouri with her husband and three children.